BARMING DURING THE SECOND WORLD WAR

LIFE IN A KENTISH VILLAGE IN THE WAR

BARMING HISTORY SOCIETY
Email: BARMINGHISTORY@MAIL.COM

BARMING DURING THE SECOND WORLD WAR

A HAPPENING PRESS BOOK:

Published by

The Happening Press
17 Vicary Way, Maidstone
Kent, ME16 OEJ
England

www.gettingyourselfpublished.co.uk

ISBN: 978-1-908137-07-4

TABLE OF CONTENTS

FOREWORD

This is the first book that has been compiled by members of the Barming History Society, which was formed in 2009 and now has over one hundred and thirty members. Needless to say, it is not possible to write a book like this without help from a large number of people.

Lesley Bellew, Linda Evans and Ian West of the Archive Department of the Kent Messenger have provided us with much help and advice. In addition they have allowed us to use some of the photographs from their enormous collection. Another source of photographs is the War and Peace Collection, Kent Photo Archive and, again, Rex Cadman has been very generous to us. Robin Halls, the headmaster of Barming Primary School arranged for us to have access to the school log which was a rich source of information. This was supplemented with help from Pip Davey.

We could not write any of this without the collaboration of many people who gave us their wartime stories. The long list includes May Pilbeam, Eileen Austin, Gerry Walters, Pamela Bennett, John Sim and his sister Pat Christen-Sim, Betty Lazell, Valerie Gooding, Hilda Smallbone, Pauline Webb, Edna Tree, David Atkinson, Daphne Sutherland and Ron Morris. Peter

1

Keith and Robin Ambrose also provided additional material.

We must also thank many people who have encouraged us to persevere with the book. In particular, Councillor Fay Gooch has helped us with advice and made a generous donation to offset some of our production costs. To all of these people we express our sincere thanks and apologise to anybody we have omitted.

We would, of course, like to hear from anybody with more information on life in Barming during the war.

Roger Birchall
Joan Howe
Barry Plummer
Ray Pyman

2

INTRODUCTION

Barming is a village in Kent some two miles west of the County Town of Maidstone adjacent to the A26 Tonbridge Road. At the time of the Second World War the population was about 1,400 and the village covered a relatively small area as can be seen from the sketch map. The population of the village increased during the 1960's with the creation of the new housing estates. These extended eastwards merging Barming with the outskirts of Maidstone. The wider Barming area now has a population of around 5,000.

All too often when World War 2 is studied in history lessons at schools the emphasis is on the wider picture of military campaigns. In this book we have tried to describe the effect of the war on our local community and the efforts that they made to carry on a 'normal' life but at the same time to support the 'war effort'. The lives of most residents were disrupted at many levels and sacrifices were made. As can be seen by the later pages of the book many made the ultimate sacrifice.

It is, perhaps, worth noting that fund raising played an important part in this support of the 'war effort' and the amounts of money raised from such a small population are truly staggering when it is realized that, to make a comparison with today's values (2011), it is necessary to multiply the amounts by between 38 and 40.

Needless to say, the war made a tremendous difference to people's lives. It caused a great deal of fear. Fear of whether their loved ones in the services would be killed or injured, fear for their own safety, fear of damage to their property during air raids and fear of the consequences of a Nazi invasion.

On a more mundane level it interrupted people's normal routines. Work, travel, schooling and leisure were all transformed by the war.

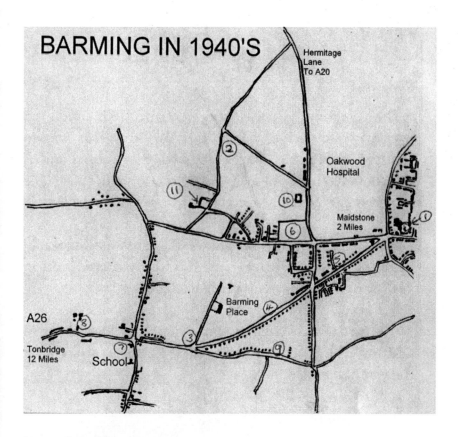

BARMING IN 1940'S

Hermitage Lane To A20

Oakwood Hospital

Maidstone 2 Miles

Barming Place

A26

Tonbridge 12 Miles

School

Key to locations on map
1 Tonbridge Road Bus Depot
2 Oakwood Hospital Cemetery
3 Site of bomb, Tonbridge Road, June 1941
4 Tonbridge Road
5 Site of Bomber Crash, 17th September, 1940
6 Barming Heath
7 Bull Public House
8 Old Hall
9 Glebe Lane
10 Nurses Home
11 Long Rede House

IDENTITY CARDS

The National Registration Act of 1939 required everybody to carry an Identity (ID) Card. This was to facilitate identifying people who had been injured and, it was hoped, it would help to detect foreign spies. The requirement for ID cards also applied to children.

There were several designs of ID cards as illustrated below. Initially they were made of brown card but, in 1943, the colour for adult cards was changed to blue.

The cards had to be updated if the holder changed address. They were in use until 1952; seven years after the war had ended.

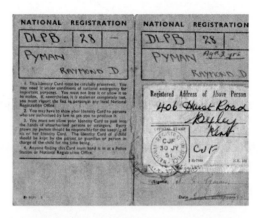

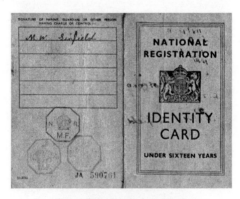

7

OFFICIAL ADVICE

There seems to have been no shortage of official advice concerning how to cope with the problems which a war was expected to cause. The number of leaflets issued was considerable. One such was the 'War Emergency Information and Instructions':-

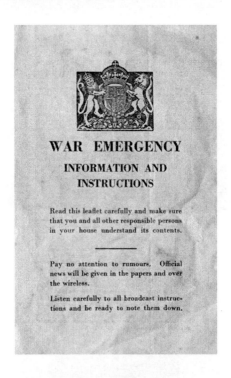

This had advice on the following subjects:-
Identity Labels
Air Raid Warnings
Lighting Restrictions

Fire precautions & Incendiary Bombs
Closing of Cinemas, Theatres etc

Instructions to Drivers & Cyclists
Travelling by Road & Rail
Telegrams & Telephones
Closure of Schools
Evacuation
Food Supplies
Payment of Pensions, Separation Allowances etc.
& National Health Insurance

The final message is:-

*'KEEP A GOOD HEART WE ARE GOING TO WIN
THROUGH'*

Another leaflet was entitled 'Hints on Household
A.R.P.' written by Mrs. Creswick Atkinson, Technical
Adviser to Women's Voluntary Services for Civil
Defence. It contains details of shelters and coping with
air-raids. A sample is shown following:-

SHELTER PREPARATIONS

Are you sure you have everything in your shelter which you will need?

Do you keep plenty of drinking water there, and something to drink out of?

Do you renew the water daily?

You probably have no idea how thirsty people get when they are frightened.

Have you put toys there for the children and books or papers for yourself?

Have you made any sanitary arrangements?

Fright has a particular effect upon people, and because of this effect, sanitary arrangements are very necessary.

So keep one or more chambers in the shelter and something to cover them with, such as a tin tray; and some toilet paper.

Keep a bottle of disinfectant there, too. People cannot run to and from the lavatory during a raid, and you will have an unpleasant job afterwards if you do not make some such arrangements.

Have you something in the shelter with which you can make a noise?

8

An old frying pan and a poker will make a marvellous noise, or a strong tin and a metal skewer. An old motor horn is even better.

In this way you will be able to let the rescuers know where you are if your entrance and exit are blocked.

Do you pack a basket or bag every morning, ready to take to the shelter with you?

And do you leave it ready at night, so that you can pick it up at once if you need it?

It should contain cold food—eating is a splendid way of passing the time, especially for children—something to drink, a tin of sweets, a First Aid outfit if you have one, a shaded torch, and anything else you may need particularly.

Do you think you should put on your gas mask directly you hear the Air Raid warning?

You should not do this unless you have heard the "Gas" Alarm.

Putting on the mask when it is not necessary will make you slower in reaching shelter. But if you are in any doubt as to whether gas is present or not, PUT ON YOUR MASK. It is better to be sure than sorry!

9

FAMILY INSTRUCTIONS

Have you made any rules for your family to follow if there is an air raid?

Here are some suggestions:

1. On going to bed, put ready a pair of outdoor shoes, a pair of stockings, or socks, a pair of knickers, or pants, a warm coat and the gas mask.

2. On hearing an air raid warning, DO NOT TURN ON THE LIGHT IF THE WINDOWS ARE UNCURTAINED.

3. Put a shaded torch ready to hand, and direct the beam down on to the floor if needed.

4. Get up quietly, without fluster. Put on the suggested clothing. OVER night-gown or pyjamas.

5. Wrap the top blankets of the bed round the shoulders. These extra covers will be a comfort in the shelter.

6. Collect the gas mask.

7. Assemble quietly ready to go to shelter.

8. Do not RUN, or get excited.

9. NEVER BE SELFISH in entering a shelter. DON'T PUSH. Pushing will make you slower, not quicker.

10

Air Raid Wardens had their own set of instructions:-

Metropolitan Borough of Paddington

WARDENS'
HANDBOOK

(First Edition)

ACTION TO BE TAKEN
BY WARDENS
BEFORE, DURING AND AFTER AN
AIR-RAID

DECEMBER, 1939.

W. H. BENTLEY,
Controller.

10

In addition, Boy Scouts were given a book of instructions.

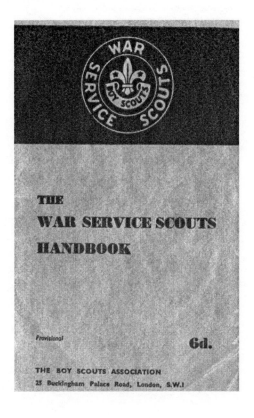

THE

WAR SERVICE SCOUTS

HANDBOOK

Provisional

6d.

THE BOY SCOUTS ASSOCIATION
25 Buckingham Palace Road, London, S.W.1

It had an interesting introduction from the Chief Scout:-

War Service Patrols - here's your book of the words. As you will see, it concentrates on those parts of Scout training that specially deal with what a Scout should know in a National emergency. Work on these lines and you will be a credit to whatever branch of the Service you join.

Scouts must live up to their motto "Be prepared", and this handbook points the way to "preparedness" for the particular job in hand.

This is a Life or Death struggle. Don't die and let others die through your unreadiness.

Yours
Chief Scout

There seemed to be a great fear of being attacked with poisonous gases following experience in the First World War. The advice given if such an attack occurred is shown following:-

6 Poison Gas. (Immediate action is always to adjust respirator.)			
Group, Name and Category.	*Means of Identification.*	*Effects.*	*First Aid.*
Choking Phosgene Non-Persistent	Invisible; smell of musty hay.	Very deadly lung irritant. Symptoms: Cough, watering eyes, difficult in breathing, pain in chest.	Fresh air. Complete rest. Warmth. No stimulants or smoking. Hot *sweet* tea. (Treat as stretcher case from start.)
Choking Chlorine Non Persistent	Greenish colour; dissolves in water; rots clothing. Smell of bleach powder.	Deadly lung irritant. Symptoms: as for Phosgene with retching and vomiting.	
Tear Various Non-Persistent and Persistent	Gaseous state almost invisible. Identified by immediate effects.	Copious flow of tears and spasms of eyelids.	Fresh air. Bathe eyes with water.
Nose Non-Persistent	On heating gives off an almost odourless smoke. Visible; produce sneezing and pain in nose.	Pain in throat and chest; vomiting; mental depression; influenza feeling, aching teeth and head.	Fresh air and tea. (Symptoms may increase owing to delayed action but RESPIRATOR must be kept on.)
Blister Mustard Very Persistent	Heavy, oily liquid, dark brown to straw colour. Penetrates materials. Neutralised by bleaching powder. (N.B.—Use only a mixture of bleach and earth or liquid mustard gas may burst into flame.) Smell of garlic or horse-radish (and appearance of liquid.)	(a) Liquid: severe inflammation of eyes; redness on skin in two hours followed by blisters in 8-12 hours. (b) Vapour: inflammation in eyes with swelling and temporary loss of sight; loss of voice and coughing; irritation and blisters in 12-24 hours.	*Liquid Mustard*—Eyes: wash with water or bicarbonate solution, and pass on to medical services. Skin: swab off surplus and apply bleach paste. Blisters: do not prick but cover with dressing. *Lewisite and Dick:* do not prick blister where no first-aid facilities exist but cover with dressing; where they do exist, prick with sterile needle, squeeze, and apply sterile dressing. *Vapour*—Eyes and Lungs: Pass on at once to medical services. Skin: wash with soap and water and change clothing.
Blister Lewisite Persistent	Oily colourless liquid giving off invisible gas. Rapidly decomposed by water. Penetrates materials. No smell when pure. In crude state gives off smell like geraniums.	(a) Liquid: in eyes immediate effect and permanent injury; on skin blisters develop rapidly. (b) Vapour: inflammation of lungs. Action on skin as mustard gas.	
Blister Dick Persistent	Colourless oily liquid; vapour affects nose and head like nose gases.	(a) Liquid: blindness; redness on skin in 1-2 hours, blisters in 4-8 hours. (b) Vapour: affects nose and head; choking and coughing.	
Arthur (or *Arsine*) Persistent and Non-Persistent	Either an invisible gas (N.P.) in bombs, etc., or a grey powder (P.) which in contact with moisture gives off the gas.	First signs are headache and fatigue. Nausea and vomiting follow. Face may turn yellow, then copper.	As for choking gases.

13

FOOD SUPPLIES AND CLOTHES

Anticipating the coming of war and probable food shortages, from June 1939 Maidstone Council sold various vegetable seeds to local residents at cost price in order to encourage people to grow their own produce in gardens and allotments.

Inevitably there were food shortages due to disruption to farming and shipments from overseas. This resulted in food rationing being introduced. Every person was given a ration book and had to register with a local grocery store. The shop was only supplied with enough food for people on their list. Upon buying rationed food, the grocer attached a sticker to the customer's ration book or marked it with an indelible pencil.

Initially only sugar, butter and bacon were included but by the summer of 1940 all meat, cheese, eggs, tea, milk and jam were rationed. One person's weekly allowance was:-

4oz lard or butter
12oz sugar
4oz bacon
6oz meat
2 eggs and 2oz tea

Some local residents concentrated on keeping poultry and received an allocation of corn which replaced their egg ration. The local food office would collect any surplus eggs.

There were no restrictions on vegetables but often there were shortages of them. Similarly, only fruit grown in the British Isles was available. In addition, dried egg powder was produced for making scrambled eggs.

Food manufacturers found it difficult to obtain supplies for their processing plants. As a result, they advertised locally for produce.

WANTED

We are open to contract for large quantities of CHERRIES, PLUMS, RASPBERRIES, LOGANBERRIES and all other kinds of fruit, delivered to either of our Factories at Barming, Paddock Wood or Faversham.

Telephone 'Barming 86134,' giving particulars, when our representative will call upon you

SMEDLEY'S
CANNING FACTORIES
BARMING

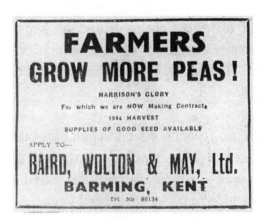

Many residents supplemented their ration by growing their own vegetables and fruit. This was encouraged by the government's 'Digging for Victory' campaign. Often slogans were used to encourage the people to participate for example:-

Dig for Victory song

Dig! Dig! Dig!
And your muscles will grow big
Keep on pushing the spade
Don't mind the worms
Just ignore their squirms
And when your back aches laugh for glee
Just keep on digging
Till we give our foes a wigging
Dig! Dig! Dig! for Victory!

Additional allotments were established at several sites in Barming including the bowling green by Bramble Close, in the Tonbridge Road just below the old Bus Depot and in Cherry Orchard Way but not on Barming Heath itself.

Several people have told us about rearing chickens and rabbits for food. When there was a surplus of eggs in the spring, they were preserved in isinglass* in a large crock, so as to supplement the dried eggs in the diet. Similarly fruit was bottled in Kilner Jars.

David Atkinson's family reared rabbits which were killed by Mrs. Featherstone in her cottage in South Street. After the dead rabbits had been hung up in the outside toilet, his grandmother came over from Old Tovil Road to skin them and prepare them for the table. On one occasion his grandmother and aunt arrived from Maidstone Market with a box with holes in it. This contained six young pullets to provide the family with eggs. Unfortunately three turned out to be males!

Locally caught wild rabbits were sold for food in the Barming Bull and it has been pointed out that the women were very inventive with their recipes as they did not want to waste anything.

*Isinglass is a pure, transparent or translucent type of gelatin. It was used for the preservation of eggs in their shells, and in glues and jellies

Following the example of groups of firemen, policemen, railwaymen and commercial enterprises, many locals with a piece of spare land jointly formed a 'Pig Club'. All discarded food, vegetable and fruit peelings, slops etc. would be collected in pails in people's kitchens to make pig swill. This was emptied into pig-bins regularly and taken to feed the 'Pig Club' animals.

The bins were placed around Barming at convenient locations by both the Council and local farmers. Oakwood Hospital sponsored some bins for making swill for their own pigs.

The Ministry of Food advertised this with the following slogan:-

Because of the pail, the scraps were saved
Because of the scraps, the pigs were saved
Because of the pigs, the rations were saved
Because of the rations, the ships were saved
Because of the ships, the Island was saved
Because of the Island, the Empire was saved,
And all because of the housewife's pail

Later in the war it became apparent that new clothing was in short supply. This was due to a shortage of raw materials and the military requirements of clothing factories to produce uniforms and parachutes.

The government had a campaign to encourage people

to 'make do and mend', but despite this, clothing rationing was introduced on 1st June 1941 and it was continued until 15th March 1949.

Everybody was issued with a clothing ration book, containing the coupons. These could be exchanged in the clothes shop, each type of clothing having a particular value in coupons. So as to stagger the purchasing of clothes, the coupons were of different colours and the government decreed when a particular colour of coupon could be used.

It was intended that the coupons would allow people to purchase one new set of clothes each year. Heavier children were issued with supplementary coupons.

Knitting wool was distributed with patterns for gloves, scarves and balaclava helmets for servicemen. Locally, Miss Maplesden-Noakes of Long Rede House organized the knitting of socks for soldiers.

1942-43 CLOTHING BOOK

This book may not be used until the holder's name, full postal
address and National Registration (Identity Card) Number
have been plainly written below IN INK.

NAME *RAYMOND DOUGLAS PYMAN*
(BLOCK LETTERS)

ADDRESS *'SHELLAND' ALEXANDRIA DRIVE*
(BLOCK LETTERS)

(TOWN) *HERNE BAY.* (COUNTY) *KENT.*

NATIONAL REGISTRATION (IDENTITY CARD) NUMBER

DLPB / 28 / —

N. R.

Read the instructions within carefully, and take great care not to lose this book

ANTI-INVASION PREPARATIONS

Early in the war, when it was feared that the Germans
might invade our country, plans were drawn up for the
evacuation of Maidstone residents to outlying areas. It
was thought that houses would be evacuated as far from
the town centre as Hartnup Street. Concrete blocks with
reinforced iron bars were to be placed across Tonbridge
Road near Milton Street and by the Cherry Tree Public
House. Residents inside this boundary received letters
indicating to which houses they were to be sent. Similarly
Barming residents received letters telling them who were
to be billeted in their houses.

20

Road blocks by the Cherry Tree Public House, Tonbridge Road (photo Kent Messenger)

May Pilbeam's mother was told that they were to accommodate a family of about ten even though their house in Barming only had three bedrooms. They were given no choice in the matter. Also they were not told what to do if invading troops reached Barming. She was glad there was no invasion!

Anti-tank blocks were made of concrete and colloquially known as 'Dragon's Teeth'. In Barming Woods there are still the remains of several anti-tank concrete blocks.

Anti-tank blocks remains in Barming Woods

Additional defences against invasion included the building of pillboxes. These were aimed mainly to protect us from invasion along the River Medway. Pillboxes were built on the banks of the River Medway and were known as the 'Ironside Line'. Those located at Barming Bridge, Barnjet in West Barming and to the East of Farleigh Lock still exist.

A recent photograph of a pillbox near Farleigh Lock. It has had a structure built on its roof and on its side

The War Department decided that, if there was an invasion, there was an area of Barming which would be suitable for an ambush of the invading army. This was in North Pole Lane at the junction of the track leading to the water tower and Ditton. The lane led to West Malling aerodrome.

Consequently, a pill-box was constructed on the South side of the lane at this point, behind the 'Wayside Cross' memorial. It still exists today in the front garden of the Wayside Cross' house but it has been covered over with earth in recent years.

FIREWATCHING

During the early part of the war, there was a great fear of incendiary bombs being dropped. This resulted in the passing of 'The Firewatchers Order' in September 1940. The order was made to compel men to fire watch for a maximum of forty-eight hours per month. Factories and businesses were obliged to appoint firewatchers to act as lookouts outside working hours.

The role of the firewatchers was to look out for incendiaries and to extinguish any fire before it could take hold. To facilitate this they were usually on duty at a high point in a town or village.

The firewatchers were each issued with a bucket of sand, a bucket of water and a stirrup pump. Apart from fighting any fires, they were required to report any fires to the appropriate authorities.

A fire engine was stationed at Old Hall, Barming just off the A26 on the Western edge of the village. Another temporary fire station was in Bower Lane. This was partly to facilitate the fighting of fires locally but also to avoid the loss of many appliances if the main fire station, in Market Buildings, off Maidstone High Street, was bombed. Pam Bennett's mother was stationed at the one in Bower Lane. The women were generally required to do office work and answer the switchboards rather than fight fires.

Barming resident Pauline Webb recalls her father being appointed a firewatcher and having responsibility, with two neighbours, for sixteen homes in West Walk, Barming. They each had two buckets, one for sand and one for water but the one stirrup pump had to be shared with the other two firewatchers.

Another Barming resident was John Sim who lived in St Andrews Road, Barming and worked at Oakwood Hospital where he was appointed a firewatcher. He recalls that he usually carried out this work from the roof of the Nurses Home in Hermitage Lane but he did not see any fires. These duties continued until he was called up for the services in 1941.

David Atkinson's father was also a firewatcher. He worked at the Diamond Fibre Works in Maidstone and lived in the house at Barming School where his wife was the caretaker. Also, Mr. Kay was the firewatcher in charge of Glebe Lane.

Daphne Sutherland told us that, as a result of fire watching duties, they got to know their neighbours better.

*A.R.P. Wardens on exercise at Barming
(Photo Kent Messenger)*

THE WOMEN'S LAND ARMY

The women's Land Army was formed in June 1939 by the Ministry of Agriculture and Fisheries in order to increase the amount of food farmers were able to grow. Initially the members were volunteers but later many women were conscripted into the organization so that there were over 80,000 members by 1944. It was officially disbanded in October 1950. The women worked long hours and the work was hard. They wore a uniform and the average pay was £1.12s (£1.60) per week.

One local resident, Pauline Webb, joined the Land Army when she was seventeen years of age. She was sent to Detling Aerodrome, about five miles to the North of Maidstone, with her friend Margaret Cook from Cherry Orchard Way and they were joined there by two London girls who were staying in a caravan. Pauline was immediately told to drive a tractor and trailer down Detling Hill to a field at the bottom and to take four other girls with her. She told them that she could not drive but the response was that this did not matter and she still had to do this. Fortunately, she succeeded in this task despite Detling Hill being tortuous and steep.

Later she worked on a farm at Haywards Heath followed by one at Ightham. Whilst at the latter her father was badly injured when the signal box at Maidstone

West station was wrecked by a doodlebug on 3rd August 1944, killing seven men and two dray horses owned by Fremlins Brewery. As a result of this she was transferred to Mays farm in Hermitage Lane, Barming. She was asked by her new employers what experience she had with farm animals and she told them that she knew how to milk a cow. Following this she was put in charge of a large Shire horse! Amongst other tasks with the horse she had to take hops to an oast house near the Tudor Garage in the London Road, Allington. Also, she remembers taking it by herself for shoeing at the Manser Forge on the Tonbridge Road, Barming just to the West of the Bull Public House. Upon returning to the farm, she passed the Fountain Inn where local children jumped on the trailer and hitched a lift.

A Barming resident who joined the Land Army was Edna Tree. She had been to Swanley Horticultural College and, in 1940, she worked on a farm in Lower Road, East Farleigh. She was in lodgings in East Farleigh and her pay was £1.8s (£1.40p) per week. Rent was £1 and insurance one shilling. The remaining seven shillings was spent on food although she remembers she always felt hungry!

Later she changed to new lodgings where the rent was only 17s.6p (88p). The landlady was very 'motherly'. On one occasion, after going to the cinema in Maidstone, she was late home. She had got onto a train to return home when there was an air raid. The train had to remain stationary during the raid. She got off the train and walked home but she was told off by the landlady for being so late upon her arrival.

Edna Tree (2ⁿᵈ from left) & friends in the Land Army
(Photo E Tree)

Having trained at Swanley Horticultural College in market gardening she mainly worked in the vegetable fields. She remembers helping to dig out old apple trees and sawing them into logs, helped by Harry Lawrence. An oast on the farm had been converted into a pigsty and Edna collected and prepared the swill.

In 1943 she moved to Canterbury in order to live with her mother.

Edna Tree   *(photo Edna Tree)*

Daphne Sutherland pointed out that when she started work for the Kent County Council in the spring of 1944 groups of volunteers would be taken by lorry in the evenings to farms. They then undertook 'stone picking' to improve the soil for growing crops. One of the areas she was taken to was Boxley. Conscientious objectors also joined these groups.

THE HOME GUARD

An appeal was broadcast on the radio on 14 May 1940 for men aged 17 to 65 who were not serving in the armed services to become part-time soldiers. Thus the 'Local Defence Volunteers' was created. It was known as 'Look, Duck & Vanish' by regular soldiers which may explain why its name was changed to 'The Home Guard' in July 1940 but later became well known as 'Dad's Army'

Within twenty-four hours a quarter of a million men had volunteered and by the end of July this had reached one million. Members included those who had essential jobs such as teachers, bank staff, and farm and railway workers. In addition, men who were too young (under 18 years) or too old (over 40 years) to join the regular army were enlisted.

The men received military training usually in the evenings. At first, they had no uniforms and few weapons. The public were requested to hand in any rifles, shot guns and pistols they had for use by the force. Within a few months twenty thousand guns had been donated. Many home-made weapons were created from knives, pieces of pipe etc.

We must not assume that the Home Guard had ineffective weapons. An example of a potent weapon of theirs is the No.76 (SIP) Grenade which replaced the earlier 'Molotov Cocktail.' It was a self-igniting phosphorous grenade which became the standard grenade of the Home Guard. It was developed to overcome the urgent shortage of available anti-tank weapons. It consisted of a glass bottle containing liquid phosphorous, benzene or naphtha and crude rubber, and had a red or green cap.

They could be thrown by hand at enemy vehicles, into buildings etc. or fired from a 'Northover Projector'. They came in sturdy wooden cases each containing twenty-four grenades. They had to be handled very carefully as is demonstrated by the following poster:-

PRECAUTIONS

A W Bombs fire instantly on breaking in air.

If fire is started accidentally, use water freely.

Store bombs (preferably in cases) in cool place, under water if possible.

Do not store near inflammable material.

Avoid storing many bombs close together if possible.

Stringent precautions must be taken to avoid cracking bombs during handling.

The caps must never be removed.

Later uniforms were provided with an armband with the letters 'LDV' on it. Ultimately they received uniforms bearing the Home Guard insignia to replace the original LDV armbands.

The task of these men was to help defend vital establishments, such as factories, and the sea shore. If there was an invasion it was hoped that they would delay the enemy advance. In addition they were involved in the capture of enemy air crew from crashed aircraft and checking people's identity cards at road blocks. They also helped to clear bomb damage, rescue those trapped after an air raid and guard buildings which had been bombed to prevent looting.

Officers and men of E Company of a Malling Battalion of the Home Guard, made up of men from Barming, Farleigh & Teston. (photo Kent Messenger)

Barming had a Home Guard contingent whose men are shown in the photograph:-

Barming Home Guard
Cpl Richard Turk (front row, 3rd from left)
Owen Crittenden (middle row 2nd from left)
(photo Kent Messenger)

The members included Pauline Webb's father, Tommy. He was working as a signalman at the railways in Maidstone. Shifts were between 6am and 2pm or 2pm and 10pm. On one occasion, she can recall Captain Roots knocking on her front door and requesting her father to help in nearby Oakwood Park. After hastily putting on his clothes, he went but it made him late for his job at the railways. His colleague Harry Holmes had to stand in for him at the signal box. Later it was realized that, as his signaling job was very demanding, he was not required to do a night shift with the Home Guard.

Another resident's father worked at Reeds Paper Mill in Aylesford. She recalls he used to take his alarm clock with him when he was on night duty with the Home Guard so that he was not late for work at 6a.m.

By 1942 enthusiasm for the Home Guard had waned largely due to the civilian population having to work longer hours. As a result of this compulsory conscription was introduced for the Home Guard from 1942.

Following the invasion of Europe in June 1944 the Home Guard was stood down from active duties on 3rd September 1944 and their weapons were returned to the WD stores.

Miss Mapelsden Noakes was a prominent local resident living in Long Rede House and was involved in many charitable activities.

Long Rede House where Miss MaplesdenNoakes lived

During the war the Barming Home Guard was conducting a quite serious exercise in the quarry off North Pole Road. Miss Noakes was on hand in a nursing capacity to render first aid in the event of any mishaps.

Blank cartridges were being used and, although 'safe', did project an amount of wadding which could hurt if fired at close quarters. Somebody fired a blank and his companion in front sustained a scorching wound to his posterior. There then followed an unseemly struggle between Miss Noakes, who was determined to have his trousers off and demonstrate her skills, and the victim who refused to bare his backside to such as she!

The final outcome was not recorded!

GAS MASKS

Following gas attacks during the First World War, there was a general fear that the enemy might drop chemical bombs in the Second World War. To provide protection against this event, everybody was issued with a gas mask by the time of the Munich crisis in 1938. People were expected to carry the masks with them at all times. They were made of black rubber. Upon inhalation, air passed through a filter to remove any chemicals. When breathing out, the air escaped around the edges of the mask.

The masks had a smell of rubber and disinfectant making them unpleasant to wear and they often caused nausea. They were delivered in cardboard boxes but many people bought more robust covers for them. The Home Guard was issued with a military type gas mask which was considered to be much better than that issued to civilians.

There were special types for young babies and for older children. Babies were to be placed in an enclosed chamber with filtered air being pumped in using hand bellows. Fortunately they were never used in earnest as they were totally dependant upon an adult pumping the air.

The masks for children had a lengthened nose-like filter so leading to the nick-name 'Mickey Mouse' or 'Donald Duck' masks. Air was inhaled through a similar filter to the adult version and exhaled through the 'Disney' nose. They had two round glass eyepieces set in metal. Gas masks had to be worn once a week for ten minutes at school. These practice drills at school became very popular when it was discovered that rude 'raspberry' noises could easily be made using the masks!

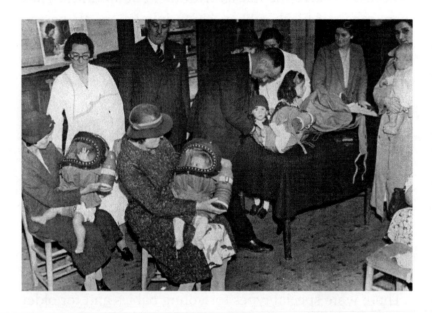

Barming parents being shown how to fit gas masks on their children.   (Photo Kent Messenger)

Child Gas Mask   *Adult Gas Mask*

BARMING SCHOOL DURING THE WAR

By the outbreak of war, Barming School had become a successful establishment in South Street having been founded in 1854. In 1939 conditions at the school were still quite primitive with oil lamps, an open coal fire and outside toilets. The war caused a severe disruption to life at the school.

Barming School, South Street, Barming

The School kept a log of activities undertaken and the following information is taken from it.

Arrival of Westborough School Children & Evacuees

On 22nd September 1939, Mrs. Hore, the headmistress of Westborough Junior School visited to discuss how Barming School could accommodate one hundred Westborough children as the result of the army using part of her own school. By 27th September the hundred juniors started at Barming, accompanied by Mrs. Hore and three assistants.

It appears that the Barming and Westborough children were to attend school on alternate days. Thus on 28th September the Barming children came but on the 29th only Westborough children were attending. This caused many problems and resulted in the schedule being changed so that only Westborough children came in the mornings with Barming children only going in the afternoons.

Children watch the guards outside Westborough School
(photo Kent Messenger)

Not all of the Westborough children were relocated to Barming as Pam Bennett attended Westborough School in 1939 and can remember having no schooling for many weeks when it was taken over by the army apart from occasional afternoons when she went to St. Michaels School further down the Tonbridge Road towards Maidstone. There they had to sit on the floor due to a lack of desks and had few books or paper to write on. It made her feel that they were 'in the way'.

By 9th October all Westborough infants had been relocated away from Barming resulting in even more confusion. As time passed more and more Westborough children were sent elsewhere so that by 12th February only one Westborough class remained with one of their own teachers. Hence Barming juniors started attending full time and only the Barming infants attending part time. On the morning of 22nd December a Christmas party was held for the Westborough children with the Barming children having one that afternoon. The remaining Westborough children left by March 1940 and a lorry collected the Westborough furniture on 8th March.

Numbers of Barming School children were increased on 23rd February 1940 with the arrival of evacuee children in Barming. Upon requesting help from the education committee at Springfield, Maidstone, the headmistress was informed that they knew nothing of these children. It resulted in 103 children being registered despite only having only 84 seats. At times there were three children to each desk and, on 11th March, a request was made for more furniture.

The whit week holiday in May 1940 was shortened to two days. This was due to the invasion of Holland, Belgium and Luxembourg by the Germans resulting in fears that the local children may need to be evacuated if England was invaded.

Preparations at the School

In June 1940 fears were expressed of the dangers of glass splinters causing injury following air raids. Having visited the school on 10th June to give a quotation, Mr. Lawrence fitted wire netted wooden frames to the windows of the main room at a cost of £10.5.0d. 'Lawrences' were a local firm of builders run by two brothers, Ronald and Phillip Lawrence and based in Heath Grove, Barming.

Unfortunately the school did not have its own air raid shelter for some time. This resulted in many parents being reluctant to let their children remain at school when the air raid sirens were activated.

As an example only seven children came to school on the morning of 30th September 1940. Because the children mainly went home at lunchtime, many did not return for the afternoon if there was an air raid warning during the day. After a few air raid warnings had occurred, the parents of the children living in Hall Cottages, Tonbridge Road, requested that their children should go home when an air raid siren was sounded until shelters had been constructed at the school. This was agreed to and the children were given homework three times a week to help make up for the missed lessons.

By January 1941 an air raid shelter had been built to house fifty children. This was situated in the area used for gardening by the children which is now part of the playing field. It resulted in all agricultural teaching being stopped. Many teachers felt this was a backward step as the children used the plot for growing vegetables! An electric light was fitted to the shelter in June 1941.

Pam Bennett remembers spending many hours in the air raid shelter. She describes how it was entered by a slope which seemed to go down a long way into a tunnel-like structure with classes situated to the right or left. Once everybody was inside there was a loud thud as the flap came down causing unpleasant feelings of being enclosed. Mothers would come to the shelters and be allowed to take their children home. If they were in the shelters for a long time, they were given Horlicks tablets.

The Disruption Caused by Air Raids

In the school log the first reference to air raids is on 5th July 1940 when many of the children were reported as being tired at school due to an air raid during the previous night. As a result the children were instructed to come to school later than normal when there had been an air raid during the night.

From September 1940 air raid warnings became quite numerous and caused much disruption at the school. The raids are recorded in the appendix. Initially, when the air raid siren was sounded the teaching ceased and the children took cover under their desks. By October 1940 it was decided that this caused too much disruption and so after that date the children continued with their classes unless gunfire was heard during a raid. There were instances of heavy raids occurring without the air raid siren being heard, for example on 13th November 1940.

On 13th June 1941 a night-time air raid caused the ceilings to fall in the main room and staff room and the window frames were smashed. Emergency repairs had been carried out by 16th June so that the school could resume its normal activities. A total of fifty-four raids were recorded by the school. It must be remembered that the total number of raids is much higher than this as these records only refer to weekdays during term time. It does, however, illustrate how disruptive they were to school activities.

As a result of the night-time blackout, the school cleaner could not get the fires going early. Thus the school opening was delayed. From 2nd February 1942, the starting time reverted to 9.00am.

Health of Children

There were several outbreaks of illnesses at the school during the war. There were regular medical inspections of the children for instance on 24th July 1940, 26th October 1941, 10th April 1942.

On 1st July 1941 a child had scarlet fever. A bigger problem occurred in March 1941 when one child had measles and twelve had whooping cough. This was followed by three more cases of whooping cough in April 1941. In April 1943 four children were absent due to mumps. Scabies was an infection which occurred in 22nd October 1942 resulting in a pupil being excluded from attending school.

Maintenance of the Buildings

The school was closed for a week from 29th January 1940 on account of the severe frost damaging the toilets and causing burst pipes. Burst pipes also occurred in January 1941 and in January 1942. Repairs were carried out by Mr. Lawrence. History was repeated in January 1944 when frozen toilets resulted in the school being closed for a week.

In July 1940 Mr. Lawrence was appointed to paint two doors and repair the locks, window panes, fences, and toilets. A new wireless set was installed in the school in April 1944. In addition two anthracite stoves were fitted in May 1944.

.

Money Raising Activities

The school raised considerable amounts of money during the war. In June 1941 the Red Cross was given 17s.6d From October 1941 to March 1942 nearly £51 was collected for National War Savings, nearly £7 for 'Warships Week' and £4 for Mr. Churchill's Red Cross fund. The 'Wings for Victory' effort in June 1943 succeeded in raising £35.4s exceeding their target of £10 by a considerable amount.

Death of a Schoolboy

During the school holidays in the summer of 1942, a local boy Geoffrey Black, aged six, was accidentally drowned in the River Medway near a hop field. When the school re-opened on 28th September 1941, the school management suggested that the owner of the hop garden should be obliged to make the river bank safe for his workers and local children.

Other School Activities

On 14th June 1943 the children were taken to Church Cross House where they were shown two films and had a talk from an R.A.F. officer.

The final event during the war years at the school was on 8th to 9th May 1945 when it was closed for a 'Victory Holiday' followed on 18th May by a victory party.

Post war, repairs to bomb damage was started in June 1945.

Further observations about the School during the War

Local resident, David Atkinson, related that his mother was the caretaker at the school during the war. At the outbreak of the war his family was living in St Helens Lane. With the start of hostilities they exchanged their house with the one at the school occupied by the headmistress Miss Pean. He spent the entire war period living in the school house.

David recalls three large elm trees in the school grounds becoming unsafe. The branches were lopped with the help of a traction engine. He also remembers that some of the children had school dinners. At first they were delivered to the school but later two cloakrooms were converted into a school kitchen.

It was hard work looking after the school. In half term the woodblock floors were scrubbed clean on Saturdays by Mr. and Mrs. Atkinson and Mrs. Manser. This took all day with them finishing the task at about 4pm.

The School Wireless

It is likely that the wireless which was installed in April 1944 was a 'Wartime Civilian Receiver'. Due to many wireless sets being destroyed by bombing, the government authorized the production of a very basic set with a plain plywood cabinet and a steel chassis.

They came in two formats, one being A.C. mains and the other battery operated, but had a common specification and they were manufactured by forty-four different companies, the only indication of the manufacturer being the serial number displayed internally. From June 1944 to May 1945 175,000 mains and 75,000 battery sets were made.

Mains model Wartime Civilian Receiver

Other Schools in the Area

It is worth bearing in mind that many other schools were disrupted with the arrival of evacuees. Pat Christen-Sim remembered that the Maidstone Girls Grammar School received so many evacuees from London that the local girls only attended school for two days on one week alternating with three days in the following week. This was, in part, due to the lack of air raid shelters. The girls were given extra homework to help them.

FUND RAISING

Many events were held, to raise funds and support the war effort particularly in the early years of the war. The war was costing the country £10 million per day (£400m in today's terms). Maidstone had many fund-raising weeks. There was a different week for each of the services and a marker on the Town Hall indicated how much had been saved. This was encouraged by visits of war heroes. Pam Bennett remembers seeing Guy Gibson, leader of the R.A.F. Dam Buster Raids, being driven through the town. He had been a member of the Boy Scout Movement before joining the R.A.F. When stationed at RAF West Malling, he had visited the Tovil Scout premises to renew his scouting promises with several colleagues who had also been scouts. Pam was disappointed that he was sitting on a chair on the back of a lorry and not in a large car!

The Kent Messenger published results for the various collections. Although some of the sums seem small, if the value of the pound is taken into account, the efforts can be seen as quite considerable. Maidstone itself raised £1million in these collections. Daphne Sutherland pointed out that, as there was so much rationing and very few fancy goods for sale, spare cash was often put into National Savings Certificates.

As the need for more aircraft became obvious in the late summer of 1940, Lord Beaverbrook, the Minister of Aviation Production, encouraged the creation of 'Spitfire Funds'. These were started all over the country and in the colonies. If £5,000 was raised, a fighter would have a local name painted on its cowling.

By the end of the war, a total of £14,000,000 had been raised nationally for these funds. In fact, many aircraft were sponsored other than Spitfires, examples being Hurricanes, Beaufighters, Blenheims, Mosquitoes and even Tiger Moth trainers. On 19th October 1940 a list of contributions to the Kent Spitfire Fund included a donation of £52.7s from the Barming Parish Church. By the end of the war the Maidstone area had raised a total of £108,451 enabling twenty two aircraft to be sponsored.

In March 1942 the paper reported that Barming had raised £3,181 in National Savings during Warship Week and in November 1942 Barming raised £87 during the Red Cross and St. John Prisoners of War Week. The money was raised with a whist drive, auction, a flag day, a poppy day and individual donations.

Barming also held a 'Salute the Soldier' week and achieved the sum of £7,324. It was noted that Mrs. Hyland of Barming Heath raised £1,500 and the children of Barming Junior School raised £66. Also an auction raised £142.10s for War Savings.

These fund raising schemes were not without criticism. Some felt that the schemes were run very inefficiently. Amongst the critics was Alderman F. Connor of Grove End, Barming Heath who wrote in the Times that there was too much 'red tape' and interference from the government officials inspecting the local collection organisation.

The government wanted to discourage people from spending on extravagant and frivolous items so as to improve the country's economy. Amongst other ways, the Squanderbug cartoon character appeared in many newspaper comic strips and short films. It had an ovoid shape with Hitler's moustache and hair style and swastikas in place of body hair.

In typical newspaper strips it could be seen sitting on peoples shoulders and whispering in their ears sayings such as 'Go and buy a new Easter bonnet, you'll look great and hats are coupon free!' or encouraging gentlemen to 'Improve your image with a new briefcase for that city businessman look'. This propaganda was so successful that its use spread to the U.S.A. and the Empire.

The Squanderbug

THE CRASH OF A GERMAN BOMBER

The 17th September 1940 was a significant date for the village of Barming during the Second World War. On that date a German bomber crashed onto houses in Barming.

It was during that night that a Junkers Ju88A1 bomber of 1/KG54 Squadron was flying from Evreux, in Northern France, to bomb the London docks. A "Boulton Paul Defiant" aircraft of B flight, part of the 141 Squadron, piloted by Pilot Sgt G. L. Laurance, made contact with the bomber, whilst flying at 15,000ft between Maidstone and Tonbridge. The air gunner on the Defiant, Sgt W. T. Chard shot at the aircraft and was assisted by ack-ack guns located at nearby West Malling airfield. As a result, the bomber disintegrated, shedding wreckage and bombs. At least seventy high explosive delayed action bombs fell in the area.

The main wreckage crashed onto a house in St Andrews Close causing considerable damage. Part of the rear fuselage landed in the gardens of numbers 410 and 412 Tonbridge Road whilst the tail section demolished greenhouses on Bellinghams Farm, in the Fant Lane area of Barming. A wing of the plane fell on St Andrews School and panels fell in local council house gardens.

By 11.40pm the ARP wardens and Home Guard members were in action putting out the fires with stirrup pumps and evacuating the area, as many incendiary bombs had been dropped by the aircraft. Women supplied the water in baths and buckets whilst the men operated the stirrup pumps. By 2.15am the fires were under control. A member of the Home Guard was quoted as saying that the stirrup pumps saved the situation. They proved to be very efficient and the local women's help was described as 'wonderful'. John Sim and his sister Pat helped to extinguish the fires in St Andrews Close with their stirrup pump using water from a fish pond.

It was discovered that a resident, Mrs. Jean Bridgland had been killed in her house which had been gutted. She was a seventy year old disabled school teacher.

In addition, the crew of the German bomber had died in the crash, three being found in the aircraft and the fourth at the rear of 3, St Andrews Close. They were Lt. Rudolph Ganzlmayr, Obfw Faschinger, Uff2 Bauer and Uff2 Schloessler and they were buried in Maidstone Cemetery three days later with full military honours.

At a later date the gutted house in St. Andrews Close was demolished.

Local resident Mrs. Pett fell into a deep hole after rushing out of her house. She was taken to hospital and treated for shock. Fortunately most residents were in air-raid shelters at the time so limiting the number of injuries.

Damage to houses in Tonbridge Road
(photo Kent Messenger)

The area was guarded during the night by soldiers until the wreckage was taken away by a Maintenance Unit lorry the next day.

Pam Bennett can remember the night of the raid. She was awake during the night and recalls a lot of noise, with many planes overhead. The next day she went to view the crashed aircraft but was not allowed near and was unable to find any fragments of the incident as souvenirs.

Gerry Walters was five years old at this time. His uncle Harold Kitney took him to the scene of the crash on his bicycle. He can remember the intense heat coming from the site. The topic of conversation amongst spectators was how lucky it was that the plane missed Mr. Hall's garage and its petrol tanks, only fifty yards away.*

Until recently this was the 'BP' garage in the Tonbridge Road which has now been demolished and is awaiting redevelopment.

Damage to houses in St. Andrews Close
(photo Kent Messenger)

CRASH OF TWO AIRCRAFT IN FANT

In 1941 a system was being developed whereby a large aircraft, carrying a searchlight in its nose, would fly with a squadron of single-engine fighter aircraft. During a raid, the searchlight would be used to illuminate the attacking bombers thereby facilitating the work of the fighters to shoot them down.

One unit testing the method was 1452 flight based at West Malling airfield. One of their aircraft was the Douglas Boston 111 twin-engine aircraft serial number W8257. On Tuesday 2nd June 1942 it was on an exercise to test the equipment accompanied by a Hawker Hurricane fighter of 32 squadron serial number Z3842. Unfortunately they collided and crashed into Fant Farm, Barming.

The pilot of the Boston P/O A. F. McManemy and the observer Sgt. G. R. Fennell were both killed. However the pilot of the Hurricane, F/Sgt. Vejlupek survived despite being seriously injured.

Following this, the police announced that two hundred cannon shells were scattered in various parts of Maidstone, especially in the Fant and Tovil areas. Anyone finding one of these shells was warned to notify the police or wardens immediately as they were liable to explode if touched.

AIR RAIDS, OTHER AIRCRAFT ACCIDENTS, BOMBS, SHELLS & DOODLEBUGS

Pam Bennett recalls that it was often difficult to sleep at night due to the air raids. Search light beams flashed across the sky picking out aircraft and there was the constant noise of ack-ack guns. These were mobile anti aircraft guns which were used in many different locations. By the morning they had always moved away. The next day the children looked for shrapnel. On one occasion she recovered some parachute silk and cord.

There were several instances of bombs being dropped in Barming. The first occasion was on the night of 10th August 1940. One hundredweight of propaganda leaflets were dropped by a German bomber onto the Oakwood Hospital area. These contained a message from Adolf Hitler. It included a translation of his speech to the Berlin Reichstag made on 19th July 1940 entitled 'A Last Appeal to Reason'.

In June 1941 a bomb landed in the area to the North of Tonbridge Road opposite Glebe Lane. It caused a massive crater and some houses in Bull Orchard were damaged with windows being broken and doors blown off. Mrs. Childs who lived opposite in Glebe Lane was injured by the bomb and had to be taken to hospital. In addition nearby fruit trees and earth were scattered all over the Tonbridge Road. Daphne Sutherland's shed door was blown off and her dog, which was sleeping in the shed, escaped into Glebe Lane. Gerry Walters went to the site next day and climbed into the crater but was soon told to leave as it was still dangerous.

A huge crater made by a bomb in Tonbridge Road
(photo Kent Messenger)

Other bombs dropped in the area in 1940 include one on the piggery at Oakwood Hospital Farm on 8th September. Also there was one on Mays Farm, Hermitage Lane Barming, 200 yards west of the nurses home, on 4th October.

Edna Tree saw a German plane crashing in Gallants Lane. This was probably the Messerschmitt Me109 serial number 14474 of 6/JH3 unit which crashed on 29th October 1940 at Lodge Farm, East Farleigh. A German airman was buried in Barming Church following a fatal crash in Farleigh. We believe it was this pilot. After the war his relatives visited his grave on several occasions before he was later transferred to a military cemetery in Staffordshire.

Maidstone suffered from being shelled by German guns located on the French coast. Two of these shells landed on the morning of Tuesday 13th June 1944 in the orchard of Hermitage Farm, Barming causing considerable damage.

Several flying bombs (V-1 Doodlebugs) fell in the Borough of Maidstone in July and August 1944. During this time six airmen were stationed in tents just to the South of Glebe Lane, Barming. When a doodlebug was sighted they used their radios to send the details to the gun sites nearer London. Also, they would fire rockets with parachute flares as an additional warning.

A flying bomb fell in open fields on Hermitage Farm on 1st July. There were no casualties but two hundred houses were slightly damaged. The last one to fall in the area crashed near Hermitage Lane in the early hours of August 3rd 1944.

On Monday 10th July 1944 a cannon shell from an allied fighter fell onto the Maidstone Corporation bus depot in the Tonbridge Road. It exploded in the concrete. At this time, a bus driver Mr. L.A. Humphries of 34 Glebe Lane, Barming was climbing the steps into the mess room. He was injured in the heel and rump and taken to hospital where he was detained.

May Pilbeam related how she was unable to sleep one night in June 1944 due to toothache. Whilst looking out of the bedroom window she saw an aircraft which she thought was on fire. It was travelling fast in a straight line and making an unusual noise. Shortly afterwards the noise stopped and she heard a loud bang. After listening to the wireless in the morning she realized that she had seen one of the first doodlebugs.

OAKWOOD MENTAL HOSPITAL

Built as the Barming Mental Asylum in 1833, Oakwood Hospital (the Kent County Mental Hospital) prepared for war prior to 1939. The staff formed squads to deal with incendiary and high explosive bomb damage and gas attacks after attending instruction at the Royal Naval Barracks in Chatham.

Air raid shelters were constructed in the grounds. For safety reasons, the upper floor of the hospital remained empty during the war so confining the two thousand patients to the lower levels in cramped conditions. Also, sandbags protected the windows and materials were applied to the windows to create a total blackout. The siren at the hospital, which previously had been used to warn of a patient escaping, was to be used as an air raid warning.

Many of the staff were called up for National Service but many trained nurses who had previously left on marriage returned to work together with refugee nurses. Sixty five members were serving in the forces by 1942 including forty four nurses. At the same time the hospital had 2214 patients being housed in accommodation intended for 1882. There were several outbreaks of dysentery, typhoid and erysipelas (a bacterial skin infection). Entertainment was provided for the patients with regular dances and a cinema on Friday nights.

Oakwood Hospital with Hermitage Lane & Nurses Home in foreground

Oakwood Hospital with St Andrews Road in foreground

There was a meeting of the Nurses League at the Nurses Home, Barming on 30 June 1940, when the new matron, Miss B. J. Wall, was welcomed by Dr. Hancock, the Medical Superintendent of the hospital. The nurses were told that Barming was the premier branch of the Nurses League in England.

Sixteen nurses were awarded certificates and eighteen staff were given badges. It was acknowledged that some staff felt that more important work was being undertaken by nurses who had gone abroad. They were told that their work at Barming was essential at a time when there were over 2,000 patients in the hospital and the Government was asking them to stay where they were in the interest of the patients and the country. Their particular skills were needed where they were, at Oakwood. Matron reminded the nurses that a patient had said that they felt safe when they saw the same nurses as 'you see the Germans shoot people like us', i.e. mentally ill patients.

Ron Morris related that his father was farm manager at the hospital farm from 1942. The Hospital grounds included a large farm of 250 acres of arable and pasture land plus a large kitchen garden. The herd of approximately fifty cows provided milk which was sent into the hospital in churns each morning and evening. There were also about two hundred pigs and two shire horses worked on the fields. In addition, by 1943-44, two Land Army girls helped on the farm and this was supplemented by German prisoners of war who came from a camp at Teston.

A slaughter house on the farm provided meat and enough vegetables were grown to supply the whole hospital. Thus the hospital was virtually self sufficient for food throughout the war.

A lack of materials hindered the occupational therapy departments. Old clothes were recycled into newer ones but, despite war time conditions, medical treatment improved during the period.

D-day was celebrated with a special church service but was followed by a period of the South East being attacked by V-1 flying bombs. The church windows and some of those of the hospital together with ceilings were damaged from nearby blasts.

Fortunately the hospital avoided major damage during the war but it was found that some of the chimney stacks and roofs had suffered damage from shrapnel and vibrations.

*Photograph taken after the Christmas Carol Concert in
Oakwood Hospital early in the war.
In front row from 4th on left Organist (C F Sim) Matron (Miss
Wall) Medical Superintendant (Dr Hancock) & the Rev Hodge
(photo J.Sim)*

BARMING MILITARY HOSPITAL

In 1938 Oakwood Hospital had been enlarged with the construction, at the rear of the main building, of Northdown House which was intended as an admission hospital. It was opened by Rt. Hon. Walter Elliot, M.C., M.P. the Minister for Health on 27th May 1938.

Before being used for their intended purpose it was taken over by the Ministry of Defence and used as a military hospital. In addition the George and Elizabeth Villas were to be used as convalescent homes for service men and women respectively. Some of the patients were housed in the bungalows in the British Legion area of Hermitage Lane. The military hospital had its own dispensary which was initially checked over by John Sim's father who was the pharmacist at the main hospital.

The following three photographs show patients being treated in the Barming Military Hospital.

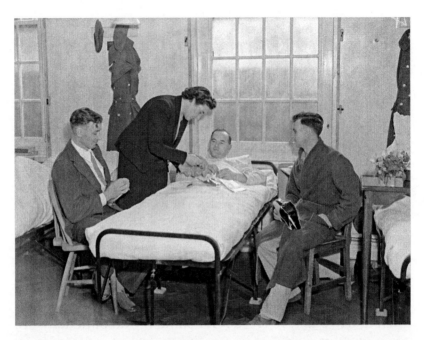

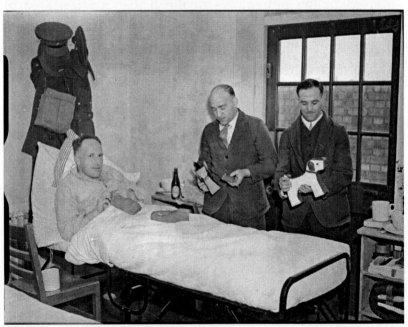

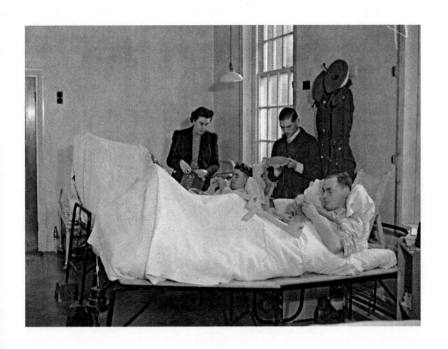

(photos War & Peace Collection Kent Photo Archive)

The 'walking wounded' soldiers were often seen strolling around the village dressed in often ill-fitting blue suits with white shirts and red ties. They frequented the tea rooms located at the back of the Heath Stores in Heath Road which was run by the two Gardiner sisters. This was next to the Duke of Edinburgh public house.

Also, the patients were regularly seen walking from the hospital, across Barming Heath to attend the hospital day centre which was located at Barming Place, in the middle of the present-day Beverley Estate

In the war years, many Polish refugees and pilots were accommodated in the hospital. Apart from injuries, others suffered from tuberculosis. This resulted in many deaths and they were buried in the Oakwood cemetery at the end of Oakapple Lane which was then known as Cemetery Lane.

BILLETING OF SERVICE MEN

Inevitably there were many soldiers billeted in local houses. Pam Bennett remembers the soldiers marching along the road and an officer coming to the door of her house to tell her mother that soldiers were to be billeted in her home. She replied that she could not have a soldier living in her house as she and her sister with three small children were alone as their husbands were away at war. He seemed to know that we had three bedrooms therefore suggested that the children could sleep with the adults, leaving one bedroom for a soldier. However, when he saw the two beds in the room, he decided that two soldiers were to be sent. Subsequently they marched into the house. Her mother had no option but was nervous at having strange men in the house.

One soldier was billeted with Eileen Austin's family in their house in Mill Walk, Barming. As a concession her mother allowed the soldier's wife and child to stay for a short while with them during the school holidays.

Amongst the servicemen billeted in Barming were many airmen from the R.A.F. aerodrome at Detling. Often they were seen cycling to Detling aerodrome each day. This must have been arduous considering the steepness of Detling Hill.

In addition to this billeted accommodation, many troops were housed in numerous bell tents along Cemetery Lane. These extended to a large area bordering on the woods.

May Pilbeam's brother was one of many Territorial Army members who enlisted in the R.A.S.C. at its depot in Union Street, Maidstone. His unit was stationed at Westborough School but he was allowed to live at home in Heath Grove, Barming.

TRANSPORT DURING THE WAR

The Maidstone Corporation bus depot was located in the Tonbridge Road, near the junction with Queens Road. In order to avoid losing all of the buses if the depot was hit during a bombing raid, the buses were scattered around the town at night. The petrol buses were kept on Barming Heath or Penenden Heath.

The trolley buses were relocated in the Tonbridge Road at night as follows:-

Two at the Fountain Inn,
One near St Andrew's Church,
One near Western Road,
One at Hartnup Street,
One at Milton Street,
and two or three near Clare Park.

Having previously worked at the Len Cabinet Works, Hilda Smallbone went on a two week course to train as a bus conductress. Despite successfully completing this, she was told that she was too young to be a conductress. This was incorrect, but she felt it was used as an excuse as they needed her to work repairing the upholstery of the buses.

She lived near to the bus depot in Barming. On many occasions, this resulted in her being woken up early in the morning by a member of the bus staff requesting her to be a relief conductress on the first bus to leave Barming at 5.15am if somebody had not turned up for work that day.

As part of the war effort, the reverse of the bus tickets included slogans encouraging people to save. The following are examples:-

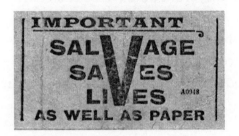

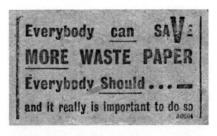

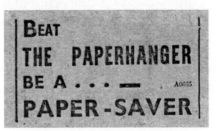

However, some advertisements were more 'pre-war':-

FUEL

Ashby's had a large coal store in Western Road. In the autumn coal would be delivered in tons but, as fuel became scarce, only 2cwt was delivered at a time.

Some things did not change during the war. Electricity & gas meters were still read every three months! A label attached to an electricity meter in the house Broumfield (formerly North House) is shown below:-

MAIDSTONE
Corporation Electricity Dept.
METER CARD.

Name...

Address...

Meter No.................... Rent...............

Supply ....

DATE	READING	ADVANCE
	6600	
5-4-4	6982	382
7-7-41	7051	69
9-1-4	7071	20
5-1-4	7472	401
1-4-42	7997	525
3-7-42	8017	20
6-10-42	8026	9
7-1-43	8092	66
2-4-43	8205	113
5-7-43	8234	29
6-43	8262	28

DATE	READING	ADVANCE
	2806	
5-2-41	2895	89
7-7-41	2720	425
6-6-41	2959	39
5/11/42	3088	129
1/0/42	3198	110
3/7/4	3219	21
6-10-42	3254	35
1-1-43	3354	100
2-1-43	3432	78
5-7-43	3451	19
5-10-43	3480	29
6-1-44	3563	83
2-4-44	3621	58
4-7-44	3636	15
1-10-44	3663	27
9/45	3750	87
9/45	3815	65
	3836	21

BARMING HEATH

A military camp was set up on the Barming Heath with the accommodation being in bell tents and, in addition, many soldiers were billeted in local houses. The Heath was used to store many army lorries and other equipment. The army provided a permanent guard to the Heath and the locals supplied them with cups of tea!

Soon after the outbreak of war, the railings around the heath and iron fencing and chains from private houses had been removed and used as scrap metal.

EMERGENCY LANDING STRIP

An emergency landing strip was located at Hermitage Lane, Barming. The actual location was approximately 500 metres north of the present day Maidstone Hospital. We have found no record of it ever being used.

VICTORY CELEBRATIONS

There were many street parties after the end of hostilities. Amongst places where they were held are Barming School, Oakwood Hospital, Bull Orchard and Glebe Lane.

The following photographs show the Victory party in Glebe Lane held on 8th May 1945.

Left 'sailor': Robbie Widows Right 'sailor': Teddy Williams
Girl foreground right: Beryl Baker
Girl background centre standing: Brenda Richardson

The pianist on the lorry is Mrs. Hodge

(photo G Walters)

(photo G Walters)

Burning an effigy of Hitler   (photo G Walters)

On Sunday 13th May 1945 a service was held at Oakwood Hospital to commemorate the victory in Europe, conducted by Rev. J. George. In addition, a party was held with a large bonfire upon which another effigy of Hitler was burned. This was held on the field which is now the car park of Maidstone Hospital.

Following the end of hostilities, all school children received a certificate from King George V1 and sometimes also from the local authority.

8th June, 1946

TO-DAY, AS WE CELEBRATE VICTORY, I send this personal message to you and all other boys and girls at school. For you have shared in the hardships and dangers of a total war and you have shared no less in the triumph of the Allied Nations.

I know you will always feel proud to belong to a country which was capable of such supreme effort; proud, too, of parents and elder brothers and sisters who by their courage, endurance and enterprise brought victory. May these qualities be yours as you grow up and join in the common effort to establish among the nations of the world unity and peace.

George R.I.

DECISIONS!

In wartime many decisions were made, some were forced on us and others were entirely voluntary. Of the latter type there can be few more poignant and life-changing than that made by Betty Lazell who is an 87 year old resident of Barming. Here is her story:

Betty in her WAAF uniform, Trafalgar Square, September 1942   *(photo Betty Lazell)*

'In March 1942 I was travelling by train from Hertfordshire to the solicitor's office in Gracechurch St. in London where I worked as a shorthand typist. The train stopped at a station and I looked out of the window at a large poster featuring a W.A.A.F. with the address of the local recruiting office. I jumped off the train as the porter was about to blow his whistle and made my way to the recruiting office. As I had passed my 18th birthday I was eligible to offer my services and was given a form to fill in. Within a fortnight I received an official letter telling me to report to an R.A.F. Station in Lincolnshire.

I then had to tell my Mum and Dad what I had done. They were upset but knew that eventually I would be called up for war work and I was not happy at the thought of going into a factory. My Mum and little brother came to see me off – they were both crying and I wondered if I had done the right thing.

I arrived at the R.A.F. Station with several other young ladies and a W.A.A.F. officer explained what we would be doing over the next four weeks and informed us that as we had volunteered we would be given a return ticket home if we did not like the sound of what was expected of us.

On completion of the training, I was posted to Headquarters Bomber Command at High Wycombe and had been there for about a year when I volunteered to become a shorthand typist at R.A.F. Balderton near

Nottingham.   Two weeks later I was on my way and found it to be an exciting place and home to Lancaster Bombers.   I worked in an office quite near the runway so my boss often allowed myself and a few others to go to wave the boys off as they boarded the aircraft.

One morning in 1944 my mate and I went across to the N.A.A.F.I. for a break and sitting on the grass were a couple of airmen. One of them waved and the other gave a rather shy smile – he was ginger haired and very good looking and had a lovely tan (he had just returned from the desert). When we came out they were just going in so we had a little chat before hurrying back to our office.

A few days later my Squadron Leader sent for me and I was told to meet a large lorry at the Motor Transport yard the next day at 0900hrs.   I was then given a large order form to hand to the Officer in Charge at an R.A.F. Stationery Store in London.   The lorry would be loaded with a large number of dead airmen's personal belongings which the driver would deliver to another store for collection by their next of kin.

The next morning I met the lorry and who was the driver? None other than the ginger haired airman I had met a few days earlier.   I looked up at the very high lorry wondering how I was going to climb up into the passenger seat as my air force blue skirt was very tight so I just hitched it up to show my frightful air force blue knickers.   As the dear driver saw my predicament he very politely turned his head away and in a very unladylike manner I fell into the seat and straightened myself out. He then introduced himself as Tom and I said I was Betty.

After driving for about two hours we stopped at a cafe for a cup of tea where the owner kindly guarded the lorry whilst we sat at a table in the window. We then made our way to the store where we had to drop off the deceased airmen's belongings. I sat in the cab whilst Tom and another R.A.F. chap unloaded everything from the lorry.

My Mother was very unhappy in Hertfordshire so by now my parents were back home in Lewisham which was our next destination. The journey was very slow as we had to keep stopping to avoid the tram passengers who had to walk to and from the middle of the road to the pavement when boarding or leaving. We eventually arrived and Tom dropped me off before making his way, in the lorry, to Woolwich where his family were living temporarily with his Grandma whilst waiting for a house in Eltham.

The following morning Tom arrived at 0930hrs and I introduced him to my Mum who made him a cup of tea. We then made our way to the Stationery Store in West London where I handed over the order I had been given. With help from R.A.F. 'bods' we finally had all the stationery loaded into the lorry and then returned to R.A.F Balderton.

I went to retrieve my bike to cycle back to the W.A.A.F. site only to find that I had a flat tyre. I turned round wondering where I could leave my bike and who should be walking along but my lovely handsome driver. He stopped when I pointed to the tyre whereupon he took the bike over to the M.T.Section, mended the tyre and brought it back to me, together with his own bike. We then cycled back to our sites – R.A.F. site on one side of the lane and W.A.A.F. site opposite. He said "how about we cycle into Newark for some fish and chips after duty tomorrow evening".   That was our first date and it turned out to be a lovely evening in every way.   We talked about our families and he told me he had never had a girlfriend before, so blushing very slightly, he asked if I would go out with him again and I said that I would be pleased to – we got on really well.

We had several more dates and then one evening we were walking in Newark when we heard a band playing so we made our way to the sound of music coming from a large Salvation Army building which bore a notice saying that all HM Forces were welcome. We went in and were greeted by a gentleman in Salvation Army uniform who showed us to a small table and asked if we would like tea or coffee – a few minutes later he returned with two big steaming mugs complete with a bun. The band was playing all sorts of wartime songs and we looked at each other and realised that there was a mutual attraction. We then had to leave in order to cycle back to camp before 2200hrs. We then did not meet for three nights as Tom was ordered to pick up some equipment needed by the M.T.Section.

Our next date was on a Saturday night and we made our way again to the Salvation Army building and were made very welcome by the same chap as before. We had tea and a bun and the next thing we knew the band started playing and the chap we had got to know came across and said this tune is just for you – 'I'll be Loving You Always'. Tom picked up my hand, kissed it and said "Yes I Will". The chap, whose name was Bert, smiled and that, was how our love affair started.

We obtained a gramophone record of that tune which we had for years and I now have a CD which the Salvation Army made with Vera Lynn.

We were married within three months of our first meeting and it was just four months before we hoped to celebrate our 60th wedding anniversary in 2005 when my beloved Tom passed away.

Most of my family live in Witham, Essex but I have one daughter and son-in-law close by. I have six grandchildren and seven great grandchildren all of whom keep in touch'.

'Thanks to the war and the R.A.F., I found the perfect husband'

POSTSCRIPT

We must not forget that these pages have not mentioned the most stressful part of life in Barming during the war. The residents' biggest worry was always the fate of their loved ones on active service away from home. The plaque in St. Margaret's Church, Barming lists the two hundred and seventy Barming residents who served in the armed services and twenty of whom were killed. Their details are also recorded as follows:-

W.BOTTEN.
Dvr. R.A.S.C.

C.G.BOTTING.
C.S.M. R.W.R.S.

C.BURNE
F/O. R.A.F.

B.H.CONNOR.B.A.
Dvr. R.A.S.C.

F.C.CURTIS.
Cpl. Royal Signals.

A.J.FISHWICK.
App. M.N.

R.C.FOSTER,
A.F/L. R.N.

S.GARGET.
Plt/Officer. R.N.

R.G.HILLS.
Bosun. M.N.

D.HOOKER.
Sgt. R.A.F.

T.H.LOVETT.
L.A.C. R.A.F.

J.L.LUCK
Gnr. R.A.

J.H.LUCKING.
Sgt. /Plt. R.A.F.

R.G.D.MATHEWS.
F/Sgt. R.A.F.

A.G.P.C.O'KILL.
Sgt. R.A.F.

J.PERKINS.
L.A.C. R.A.F.

C.T.D.SHEPPARD.
Cpl. R.A.S.C.

E.A.TURNER.
Pte. 1/4 Hampshires.

G.S.A.TUITE-DALTON.
Lieut. 6th D.C.O. Lancers, Indian Army.

S.C.WISE
Plt/Officer. R.A.F.

99

William Leslie Botten
Driver, 516 Div. Comp. Coy. Royal Army Service Corps.
Died 10th September 1943 aged 33

Cyril George Botting
2nd Battalion, Queen's Own Royal West Kent Regiment.
Died 17th April 1945 aged 33

Colin Burne*
207 Squadron, R.A.F. Volunteer Reserve.
Died 28th July 1943 aged 20

Brian Harvey Connor
23 Div. Supply Column, Royal Army Service Corp
Died 27-28 May 1940 aged 24

Frederick Clarence Curtis
2nd Armoured Brigade Signal Squadron, Royal Corps of Signals.
Died 8th September 1943 aged 35

Arthur John Fishwick
Apprentice S.S. Goolistan, Merchant Navy.
Died 23rd November 1942 aged 19

Ronald Charles Foster
Air Fitter, H.M.S. Goshawk, Royal Navy.
Died 17th January 1941 aged 21

Sydney Garget*
Ptty Officer, Royal Navy H.M.S.Curacoa
Died 2nd October 1942 aged 37

Robert Golding Hills*
Boatswain, Merchant Navy
Died 2nd December 1940 aged 52

Donald Hooker*
114 Squadron, Royal Auxiliary Air Force
Died 26th September 1940 aged 21

Thomas Henry Lovett*
Leading Aircraftsman, R.A.F.
Died 18th August 1940 aged 40

John Lionel Luck
Gunner, 112 (The West Somerset Yeomanry) Field
Regiment, Royal Artillery
Died 18th September 1944 aged 38

John Harold Lucking*
Sergeant (pilot) 142 Squadron, R.A.F.
Died 30th November 1941 Aged 21

Richard Granville Douglas Mathews
Flight Sergeant, 51 Squadron, R.A.F. Volunteer Reserve.
Died 6th September 1942 aged 21

Percy Cyril O'Kill*
Sergeant (Air Gunner) 10 Squadron, R.A.F. Volunteer Reserve
Died 7th September 1943 age21

John William Fraser Perkins*
Leading Aircraftman R.A.F.
Died 6th April 1945

Cyril Theodore Douglas Sheppard
Corporal, Royal Army Service Corps.
Died 14th February 1941 age 20

Edward Arthur Turner
Private 1/4th Battalion, Hampshire Regiment.
Died 17th October 1943 age 26

Godfrey Stuart Alan Tuite-Dalton
Lieutenant 6th Duke of Connaught's Own Lancers (Watson's Horse)
Died 17th December 1943 age 21

Stanley Cuthbert Wise
Pilot Officer 44 Squadron, R.A.F. Volunteer Reserve
Died 11th September 1940 Age unknown

In addition, another serviceman from Barming was killed on active service but he is not recorded on the war memorial or on the plaque in Barming Church. He is Flying Officer Walter John Trice.*

see appendix 1

APPENDIX 1
Details of some of those who died

Colin Burne

Colin was the son of Albert and Dorothy Burne and was aged twenty when he died on the night of 28th July 1943. He was in an Avro Lancaster 1 of 207 Squadron R.A.F., serial number W4962. It was shot down on a bombing mission to Hamburg. The pilot of the German night fighter that attacked them was Maj Walter Ehle. The plane crashed at Glinde a town approximately twelve miles East of Hamburg. Five of the crew were killed and two survived as prisoners of war. He is buried in the Becklingen War Cemetery.

Sydney Garget

Before the war Sydney lived at 19, Glebe Lane, Barming. He was on H.M.S. Curacoa when she was escorting the R.M.S. Queen Mary, which was carrying 15,000 U.S. troops across the Atlantic. His ship was a light cruiser and the ships were taking a zig zag course to try to avoid being attacked by German submarines. Unfortunately, whilst turning the Queen Mary collided with the naval ship, which was seriously damaged and sank shortly afterwards. Only 26 sailors survived but 338 drowned including Sydney Garget. This occurred on 2nd October

1942.

Robert Golding Hills

Robert was a boatswain on the Motor Tanker M.V. Ross. This was owned by the British Mexican Petroleum Company and was operated by the Ministry of War Transport. It left Liverpool in ballast for New York on 2nd December 1940 in convoy OB251 accompanied by thirty three other ships. The ship was torpedoed by the German U-boat U43 when 355 miles South West of Bloody Foreland in County Donegal. The master, all forty two crew and one gunner perished.

Donald Hooker

Donald was a sergeant in 114 Squadron R.A.F. (Auxiliary Air Force) based at Oulton in Norfolk. On 26th September 1940 he was in a Blenheim bomber attacking the channel ports. His aircraft crashed in the English Channel killing all three on board.

Thomas Lovett

Thomas Lovett was born at Plaxtol in 1900; He had worked at Oakwood Hospital as a second hall porter for fourteen years before joining the R.A.F. soon after the outbreak of war.

At 13.30 hrs on Sunday 18th August 1940, R.A.F. Biggin Hill experienced its first major bomb attack of the war. About sixty Heinkel 111 bombers of Bomber Geshwader No.1 bombed the airfield from twelve to fifteen thousand feet, accompanied by forty Messchermitt Bf 109 fighters. There were direct hits on the motor transport buildings and near the anti aircraft guns, resulting in the death of

two people, including Thomas Lovett, and injuring three others. There was extensive damage to other parts of the airfield.

Thomas was buried in the Oakwood Hospital Cemetery off Cemetery Lane (now Oakapple Lane) in Barming. His funeral was conducted by Rev. H.A. Hodge, Chaplain to the Hospital with Mr. F. Sim the organist. His widow was Daisy Lovett who died on 7th September 1993.

Thomas Lovett's grave, Oakwood Cemetery

John Harold Lucking

John was the son of Harold and Edith Lucking. He was a sergeant pilot with 142 Squadron in the R.A.F. Volunteer Reserve.

On the night of 30th November 1941 he was in the Vickers Wellington bomber serial number Z1292 flying from Waltham, just South of Grimsby. It was shot down on a raid to Hamburg. All six of the crew were killed and are buried in Kiel War Cemetery.

Percy O'Kill

Percy was a sergeant (air gunner) in 10 Squadron R.A.F. Volunteer Reserve. He was in the Halifax bomber serial number DT791 on 16th April 1943 when it crash landed near Lewes in Sussex after being hit by flak whilst returning from a raid to Pilsen. He survived this.

On 7th September 1943 he was aboard the Halifax JD166 on a mission to bomb Munich. The plane was shot down by German night fighters and crashed at Kaufbeuren. Two of the crew, including Percy were killed and the remaining five crew members were prisoners of war.

John William Fraser Perkins

John was a leading aircraftman in the R.A.F. He was captured in Java and arrived at the Sandakan prisoner of war camp in Borneo in April 1943. This camp was notorious as 6,000 Javanese civilians and prisoners of war were forced to build an airfield there. He died there on 7th April 1945. The Japanese recorded that he died of Malaria.

Walter John Trice

Walter was the son of Walter and Elsie Trice of Mill Walk Barming and he was a member of the R.A.F. Volunteer Reserve. He died on 3rd March 1945 aged twenty two.

On that day he was flying in Avro Lancaster 1 bomber serial number ME781 of 1651 HCU (heavy conversion unit). Following an operation involving a mass bombing strike against Germany and Norway, their aircraft crashed when coming into land at their base at Woolfox Lodge five miles North of Stamford in Lincolnshire. Six of the seven crew on board were killed, including Walter Trice. He is buried in the graveyard of Barming church.

Walter Trice's grave, Barming Church

APPENDIX 2
Air Raids recorded in the School Log

Year	Month	Day	No of Raids
1940	JULY	5	1
1940	SEPTEMBER	30	2
1940	OCTOBER	1	1
1940	OCTOBER	2	5
1940	OCTOBER	4	1
1940	OCTOBER	8	1
1940	OCTOBER	9	2
1940	OCTOBER	10	2
1940	OCTOBER	11	3
1940	OCTOBER	15	1
1940	OCTOBER	17	3
1940	OCTOBER	24	1
1940	OCTOBER	25	2
1940	OCTOBER	31	1
1940	NOVEMBER	1	2
1940	NOVEMBER	5	2
1940	NOVEMBER	13	1
1940	NOVEMBER	26	1
1940	NOVEMBER	29	2
1940	DECEMBER	3	1
1941	JANUARY	6	2
1941	JANUARY	7	3
1941	JANUARY	15	1

1941	JANUARY	21	1
1941	JANUARY	28	1
1941	JANUARY	29	1
1941	JANUARY	30	1
1941	JANUARY	31	1
1941	FEBRUARY	2	1
1941	FEBRUARY	4	1
1941	MARCH	18	1
1941	MARCH	19	1
1942	JULY	28	1
1942	OCTOBER	27	1
1944	FEBRUARY	16	1
1944	JUNE	16	1

BIBLIOGRAPHY

A History of Oakwood Hospital—Kent County Council

Gifts of War published by Air Britain

Out of the Blue by Anthony Webb

A History of Barming School 1854-2004

Kent Messenger Newspapers

Kent Messenger World War Two digital archive

Kent Airfields in the Battle of Britain by KAHRS

Kent Home Guard A History by K R Gulvin

Kent & the Battle of Britain by Robin Brooks

Lightning Source UK Ltd.
Milton Keynes UK
UKOW030621240911

179180UK00001BA/2/P